T0275339

SPIDERS' SECRETS

FIRST EDITION
Project Editor Caroline Greene; **Art Editor** Rebecca Johns; **Senior Art Editor** Cheryl Telfer;
Series Editor Deborah Lock; **US Editor** Regina Kahney; **Production Editor** Sean Daly;
Picture Researcher Jo Haddon; **Jacket Designer** Natalie Godwin; **Publishing Manager** Bridget Giles;
Indexer Lynn Bresler; **Natural History Consultant** Paul Hillyard; **Reading Consultant** Linda Gambrell, PhD

THIS EDITION
Editorial Management by Oriel Square
Produced for DK by WonderLab Group LLC
Jennifer Emmett, Erica Green, Kate Hale, *Founders*

Editors Grace Hill Smith, Libby Romero, Michaela Weglinski;
Photography Editors Kelley Miller, Annette Kiesow, Nicole DiMella; **Managing Editor** Rachel Houghton;
Designers Project Design Company; **Researcher** Michelle Harris; **Copy Editor** Lori Merritt;
Indexer Connie Binder; **Proofreader** Larry Shea; **Reading Specialist** Dr. Jennifer Albro;
Curriculum Specialist Elaine Larson

Published in the United States by DK Publishing
1745 Broadway, 20th Floor, New York, NY 10019

Copyright © 2023 Dorling Kindersley Limited
DK, a Division of Penguin Random House LLC
22 23 24 25 26 10 9 8 7 6 5 4 3 2 1
001–333856–May/2023

A catalog record for this book
is available from the Library of Congress.
HC ISBN: 978-0-7440-7106-1
PB ISBN: 978-0-7440-7107-8

DK books are available at special discounts when purchased in bulk for sales promotions, premiums,
fundraising, or educational use. For details, contact: DK Publishing Special Markets,
1745 Broadway, 20th Floor, New York, NY 10019
SpecialSales@dk.com

Printed and bound in China

The publisher would like to thank the following for their kind permission to reproduce their images:
a=above; c=center; b=below; l=left; r=right; t=top; b/g=background

Alamy Stock Photo: blickwinkel / G. Kunz 27, blickwinkel / H. Bellmann / F. Hecker 26bl, 30, Jack Perks 26tl,
Hakan Soderholm 28clb; **Dorling Kindersley:** Neil Fletcher 7cla; **Dreamstime.com:** Isselee 7cra;
Getty Images: Oxford Scientific 28br, Moment Open / Rundstedt B. Rovillos 42; **naturepl.com:** Emanuele Biggi 16–17b,
Stephen Dalton 33, 38inset; **Shutterstock.com:** Zety Akhzar 41tr, Art Sublimina Photography 12, Artush 13, asawinimages 17tr,
Cornel Constantin 19, DNetromphotos 7crb, Susilo Hendro 32crb, Mark_Kostich 25crb, lighTTrace Studio 21tr, Roberto Michel 37,
Sari ONeal 24–25, Rithwick Pravin 9, Peter Waters 7bl, withthesehands 11

Cover images: *Front:* **Dreamstime.com:** Teh Soon Huat b, Isselee tl, Maxborovkov tr; *Back:* **Shutterstock.com:** chekart cra,
Macrovector cla, VectorShow cl

All other images © Dorling Kindersley
For more information see: www.dkimages.com

For the curious
www.dk.com

SPIDERS' SECRETS

Richard Platt

Contents

World-Wide Web

Spiders are everywhere.
There are more than 30,000
different kinds living around
the world. Find out about
the amazing
secret lives of
six different
spiders. Watch how
one tiny spider spins
its sticky web, which can
catch a much bigger
insect for supper. Discover
how spiders adapt
to living in all sorts
of conditions—even
underwater.

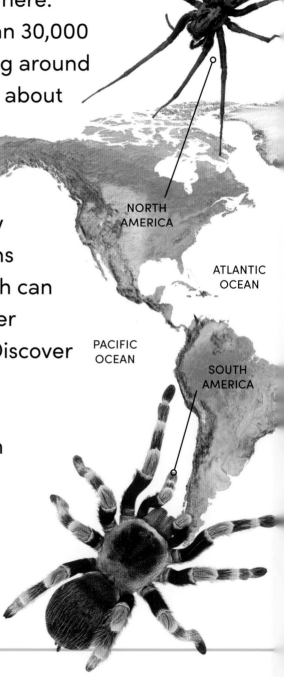

NORTH
AMERICA

ATLANTIC
OCEAN

PACIFIC
OCEAN

SOUTH
AMERICA

Tarantula: I thrive
in tropical rainforests.
Meet me on page 14.

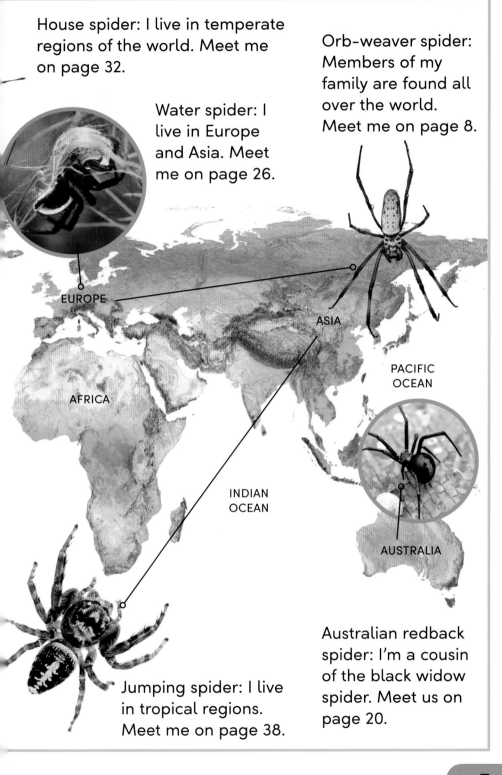

House spider: I live in temperate regions of the world. Meet me on page 32.

Water spider: I live in Europe and Asia. Meet me on page 26.

Orb-weaver spider: Members of my family are found all over the world. Meet me on page 8.

EUROPE

ASIA

PACIFIC OCEAN

AFRICA

INDIAN OCEAN

AUSTRALIA

Australian redback spider: I'm a cousin of the black widow spider. Meet us on page 20.

Jumping spider: I live in tropical regions. Meet me on page 38.

All in a Spin

orb-weaver spider

Spinning a new web is hard work for me, but it's fun to watch for you. You'll see me at my busiest early on a misty fall morning in a field or park. I am an orb-weaver spider and my web is a clever trap. "Orb" means a ring or circle, which describes my web's shape. The fine silk threads are coated with sticky goo to snare my insect food. Dewdrops on my web help you see the threads.

There are many different orb-weaver spiders. This one signs its web with a zigzag.

Some orb-weaver spiders have dotted patterns on their backs.

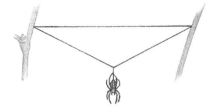

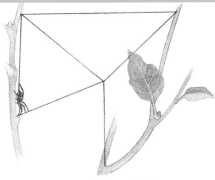

1. To make my web, I fix the first thread between two twigs. I tighten the thread and spin a looser one below. From its middle, I lower myself down.

2. I fix the thread that lowered me to a twig below. Then, I run up and down, adding to the web to make a kind of frame.

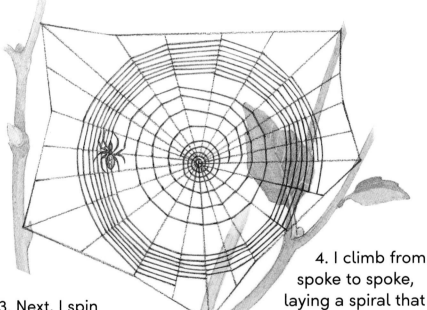

3. Next, I spin threads from the center, out to the edges. These look like the spokes of a wheel.

4. I climb from spoke to spoke, laying a spiral that adds strength. Then, I lay another spiral coated with gluey drops to make the web sticky.

If webs lasted forever, it would be an easy life, but lots of things spoil them. Rain, wind, and animals break webs. Dust takes the stickiness away. So each day, I have to start building and repairing my web again! Luckily, not all of my effort is wasted. I can eat up the threads and recycle them into fresh silk, which I spin from the spinnerets on my back.

But please don't touch our webs unless you are a fly. Then, you are VERY welcome!

Superstrong Silk

Spider silk is pulled from a spider's spinnerets. Spider silk is twice as strong as steel of the same thickness. Yet the silk is very light. A thread around the world would weigh just 12 ounces (340 g).

spinnerets

orb-weaver
spider with
dragonfly prey

Once my trap is set, I rest and wait. I cannot see much because I have bad eyesight, but I have a very good sense of touch. I can feel when my net catches an insect.

I scurry into action and reach my victim in a few seconds. To stop my meal from wriggling, I wrap it up in silk. Then, I kill it with a single bite. Dinner is served! I crush the insect's body with my jaws and squirt in digestive juice. Before long, everything inside has turned to insect soup, which I can drink. **Delicious!**

Senses
Most spiders have bad eyesight, but they sense vibrations when something lands in their webs.

Big and Hairy

We tarantulas come from a big family. Mostly you'll find us in North and South America, but we have cousins in Africa and Australia, too. We're the world's biggest spiders—my legs could stretch right across a dinner plate.

(Above) The baboon spider is an African tarantula. (Below) Tarantulas are very hairy spiders.

Dancing Cure
People in Italy used to think that you could cure a tarantula bite by performing a wild dance called the tarantella.

There is a kind of hairy spider that lives near Taranto in Italy. Nowadays, it is known as the wolf spider, but it used to be called a tarantula, after the town. When Italians first went to live in the Americas, they called the hairy spiders there tarantulas. So, that's how we got our name.

Wolf spider from southern Italy

Like other spiders, I spin silk, but I don't need a web to catch food. All I have to do is wait for lunch to walk past my burrow, and then I pounce. I catch mostly crickets, beetles, and other insects. Sometimes I eat bigger animals, such as mice or snakes.

Fearsome Fangs

Most spiders' fangs close like pincers, but a tarantula's fangs point straight down like daggers.

My Australian cousins live on small birds and bats. We can kill these creatures because we have special fangs that stab. But I wouldn't attack you unless you frightened me. My bite doesn't kill you, but it does make you very sore.

A Peruvian tarantula eating a lizard

Tarantula

I'm big and hairy, aren't I? The hairs keep us warm and protect us. They sense vibrations when enemies are close.

This hairy skin was new yesterday. I have to change it often, because I quickly grow out of it. When I feel cramped in my skin, I pump myself up so that it cracks. I pull myself out, and there's a new skin underneath. It is called molting, and it's like pulling fingers out of a glove. I can't defend myself while I do it, so I seal up my burrow with silk to keep out enemies.

A tarantula pulling itself out of its old skin

Watch Out, Dad!

Let me introduce myself.

I am a female black widow spider. Would you like me to explain my strange name? All in good time. I have other things to tell you.

I live in Arizona where the gardens swarm with delicious insects. Spiders just like me live in southern Europe and Australia, too.

We have shiny, black bodies with red markings. You will have to look hard to see them, though, because I am tiny. I would easily fit on the smallest coin. Despite my small size, I am very famous. I am one of the most poisonous spiders in the world.

The Australian redback spider has a red hourglass shape on its body.

Deadlier Than the Male
Female black widows are much bigger than their mates. The bite of the male spider is never deadly to people.

My poison is 15 times stronger than a rattlesnake's. It harms large animals, but don't worry! I rarely kill humans. We bite when we are in danger of getting squashed.

A black widow spider climbing into a plant pot

Fight the Bite
A doctor can give an injection of drugs, called antivenins, to fight the black widow spider's poison.

Poisonous spider bites are rare. My bite may not be felt at first, but soon the person would be sweaty and feeling sick, their muscles would ache, and they would feel breathless.

I am shy, and I live in dark places, like empty boxes, cans, or pots. Shoes make nice nests. So shake that shoe. And watch where you are sitting!

I was going to tell you how I got my name. The black part is obvious. And the widow? Well, I have an unusual appetite.

A widow is a female whose husband has died. To lay eggs and produce more spiders, I need to find a male to mate with. Mating makes me hungry, and a male black widow is a tasty snack. So, I sometimes eat my partner.

It seems cruel, but I'm only thinking of the children. At least their dad gives them a good start in life by feeding their mother!

Black widow spider with eggs and young

Super Scuba

I am a male water spider. I spend almost all my time beneath the surface of a pond. Other spiders live near water, but they are not true water spiders. Many can walk on water. Some can dive. One spider splashes with its legs to attract fish. But I live under the water. Breathing isn't a problem because I carry an air supply, like a human scuba diver.

A water spider traps air in a bubble so that it can breathe.

Air bubbles turn the spider's body silver.

I swim to the surface and push my bottom out. Air sticks to the hairs on my body and becomes a bubble. I take this bubble with me and breathe the trapped air when I dive down again.

I build my web under the water, too, on water plants. I don't use the web to trap food. Instead, I use it as a nest and fill it with air. To do this, I swim to the surface and catch a large bubble between my back legs. It is bigger than the bubble I use for breathing. Then, I carry it to my nest, using threads of silk to pull myself down. The web turns silver as it fills with air. Oxygen gas from the plants keeps the air fresh.

A male water spider inside his air bubble

A water spider catching a fish

Scientists call this spider *Argyroneta* (AR–gee–ro–NET–a), a name made from Latin words that mean "with a silvery net."

I live underwater because of all the food there. I eat shrimp, the young of insects, and tiny fish. I'm a hunter! If a tasty snack comes within reach, I dart out and capture it. I kill it with a bite from my poisonous fangs. Then, I carry my catch back to my nest. To feed, I use my digestive juice to turn my victim's body to liquid. Why do I go home for meals? Because the water would wash away the liquid. I don't lose a drop in my nest.

In spring, I look for a female spider to start a family. When I find her, I build a new nest next door. I spin a web tunnel, linking the two nests. Then, I scurry through to mate.

The female does not lay her eggs immediately. First, she builds an air-filled nursery on top of her own nest. Next, she lays her eggs inside a special white bag. Then, she seals the entrance with silk. Her spiderlings hatch out nearly a month later. They breathe air that is trapped in the nursery until they grow big enough to make nests of their own.

Tiny Swimmers
Male water spiders are a little bigger than females: a pair would fit easily on a postage stamp.

Spiderlings in the nursery

House Guests

I remember you! You tried to step on me, but you weren't quick enough. House spiders like me are the fastest sprinters on eight legs. We are great travelers, too. When people first sailed from Europe to America, we went with them. Now we have family all over the United States and Europe.

house spider

Soaked Survivors
House spiders can survive a soaking in cold water. Though it might look like they've drowned, they will be fine once they dry out.

If you find a spider in your bathroom, it will not be a female like me. We stay close to the web. No, it will be a male house spider. Some spiders have hairy feet that grip shiny slopes, but a house spider does not. He loses his grip on the surface of a bathtub, slides in, and cannot escape. Don't scream and run from the room when you find him. He won't harm you. Just drape a towel over the edge, and he will climb out.

In case you forget that I share your house, I leave cobwebs as little reminders. You may think my webs are dirty, useless things, but to me, each one is home sweet home. All right, I admit my web is a mess, but it catches flies just as well as the prettiest orb spider's web.

A male house spider catching a fly

Do you know how something so fine as my cobweb can last for years? It's because I coat each thread with chemicals to keep the silk from rotting. The chemicals are antibiotics, like the drugs your doctor sometimes gives you when you are sick.

Of course, nobody wants cobwebs everywhere. They gather dust and make a house look dirty. But think before you get out the vacuum cleaner. Do you really have to clear away ALL my webs? If you leave a few, I will work hard for you. I will guard your house against other spiders that can give you nasty bites. (I keep them out by eating their food and by taking the best places to build webs.) I will catch the flies that spread germs, too.

A house spider eating its prey

My webs also trap furniture beetles, which you call woodworms. I do all this as well as any insect spray, and I do it without any harmful chemicals and free of charge!

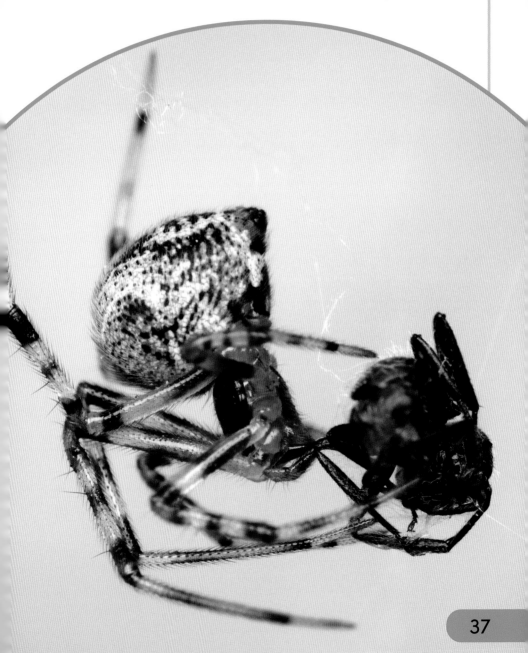

Jumping Jack

Keep still! I have spotted a cricket. If you don't scare it, I will soon have a delicious snack. Most spiders wait for their meals to walk by, but not me. I go out hunting high in the trees of the rainforest.

Olympic Leaper
Some jumping spiders can leap 40 times their length. If they were human, they'd be able to clear three tennis courts.

I am called a jumping spider because that is how I hunt. When I see something tasty, I creep toward it with the stealth of a cat. I wait. Then, I spring! Before I leap, I spin out a safety rope of silk, just in case I miss my target. But I don't miss very often.

These are two photographs joined together to show how the spider leaps onto its prey.

To spot my victims, I need sharp eyes
and lots of them! I have eight altogether.
The three smaller pairs give me all-around
vision. I can spot danger ahead, behind,
and on both sides, all at once.

The two headlights at the front are my hunting eyes. They are super sharp. They let me see in three dimensions and in color, just like your eyes. You will see them change color as I look around. When they turn black, that means I am looking straight at YOU!

My bright markings make me one of the most colorful spiders in the world. Surely, even you find me hard to resist? However, not all male jumping spiders are colored like parrots. Many of us are quite drab. And some of us are brilliant mimics. For instance, a few of my cousins look like leaves and twigs. You would never spot them on the rainforest floor.

We also disguise ourselves as beetles and ants. It's a clever way to avoid being eaten by birds. Spiders are tasty, but the ants and beetles we imitate taste horrible, so birds leave us alone.

A jumping spider disguised as an ant

A multicolored jumping spider

Male (left) and female (right) jumping spiders

When it is time to find a mate, I start the same way every spider does. I follow my noses! Yes, NOSES, for I have many of them. I sense smells through lots of tiny holes on my legs. A female spider leaves her scent on a thread of silk, which she spins as she moves.

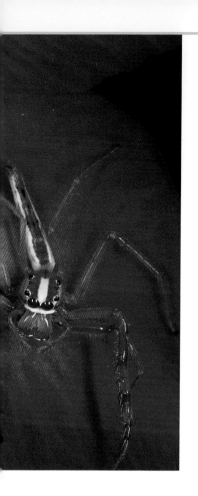

When I sniff her silk, I know I am on her trail. Once I have tracked her down, I start to dance. I wave my front legs in the air and run sideways. Soon, she is under my spell.

Jumping spiders come in many shapes, colors, and sizes.

Glossary

Antibiotic
A healing drug

Antivenin
A drug that fights the effects of a poisonous bite

Cobweb
A silk web that a spider makes to use as a trap or a home

Cricket
A long-legged jumping insect

Dewdrop
A drop of water that collects on cool objects at night

Digestive juice
The fluid that animals produce to turn solid food into a liquid, which their bodies can absorb

Disguise
A color or shape that helps an animal fool other creatures

Fang
A long, pointed, sharp tooth

Molt
To throw off an outer skin and replace it with a new one that has grown underneath

Nursery
A special room for babies; a web made for raising baby spiders

Orb web
A web that has a circular shape

Oxygen
A gas found in air and water that all animals need to stay alive

Poison
A chemical causing illness or death

Prey
An animal hunted or captured for food by another animal

Scuba
A tank of air and a face mask that allows divers to breathe underwater; water spiders create their own scubas by using an air bubble

Silk
A fine thread produced by spiders and some insects

Spiderling
A baby spider

Spinnerets
The body parts that spiders use to make silk for their webs

Spoke
A thread linking the outside of a web to its center

Temperate region
Area with a climate that is neither very hot nor very cold

Tropical rainforest
A thick forest in a warm, damp region near Earth's equator

Vibration
A shaking or quivering

Index

Quiz

Answer the questions to see what you have learned. Check your answers in the key below.

1. How many kinds of spiders are there?

2. How does an orb-weaver spider know when an insect lands in its web?

3. What is the world's largest kind of spider?

4. How do tarantulas kill their food?

5. What is one of the world's most poisonous spiders?

6. How do water spiders breathe?

7. How can house spiders protect your house?

8. How does a jumping spider find its food?

1. More than 30,000 2. It can feel the insect 3. A tarantula
4. With stabbing fangs 5. A black widow 6. They trap air in a bubble
7. They eat other spiders that can bite you, as well as flies and other insects 8. With its eight eyes